GETTING TO KNOW
THE WORLD'S
GREATEST COMPOSERS

LUDWIG VAN BEETHOVEN

WRITTEN AND ILLUSTRATED BY MIKE VENEZIA

CONSULTANT

DONALD FREUND, PROFESSOR OF COMPOSITION, INDIANA UNIVERSITY SCHOOL OF MUSIC

CHILDREN'S PRESS®
A DIVISION OF GROLIER PUBLISHING
NEW YORK LONDON HONG KONG SYDNEY
DANBURY, CONNECTICUT

W9-BDX-459

Picture Acknowledgments
Music on the cover and title page, Stock Montage, Inc.; 3, portrait of Ludwig van Beethoven by Ferdinand Schimon. Beethoven House, Bonn, Germany, photograph © Erich Lessing/Art Resource, NY; 6, Schmadribach-waterfall in the Lauterbrunn Valley, Germany, by Joseph Anton Koch. Museum der Bildenden Kuenste, Leipzig, Germany, photograph © Erich Lessing/Art Resource, NY; 8-9, Prise du Palais des Tuileries, cour du Carrousel le 10 Aout 179.2, Versailles Chateau, by Jean Duplessi-Bertaux, Giraudon/Art Resource, NY; 14, The Bettmann Archive; 15, *A View of Vienna from the Belevedere*, by Bernardo Bellotto, Kunsthistorisches Museum, Vienna; 18, 19, The Bettmann Archive; 22 (both photos), used with permission of Beethoven Haus, Bonn, Germany; 23 (top) Archiv für Kunst und Geschichte, London; 23 (bottom), German Information Center, New York; 26, Archiv für Kunst und Geschichte, London; 28-29; *Landscape with Mountains*, by Caspar David Friedrich, Pushkin Museum of Fine Arts, Moscow, Russia, Scala/Art Resource, NY

Project Editor: Shari Joffe
Photo Research: Jan Izzo

Library of Congress Cataloging–in–Publication Data

Venezia, Mike.
    Ludwig Van Beethoveen / by Mike Venezia.
      p.   cm. -- (Getting to know the world's greatest composers) Summary: Briefly recounts the life of a composer who wrote beautiful sonatas and symphonies despite tragic personal problems.
    ISBN 0-516-04542-3 (lib. bdg.) – ISBN 0-516-20069-0 (pbk.)
    1. Beethoven, Ludwig van, 1770-1827--Juvenile literature.
    2. Composers--Austria--Biography--Juvenile literature.
    [1. Beethoven, Ludwig van, 1770-1827. 2. Composers.]
    I. Title. II. Series: Venezia, Mike.
    Getting to know the world's greatest composers.
ML3930.B4V46 1996
780' .92--dc20
                                   95-40234
                                   CIP
                                   AC MN

Copyright 1996 by Mike Venezia.
All rights reserved. Published simultaneously in Canada.
Printed in the United States of America.
    9 10 R 05 04 03 02 01

A portrait of Ludwig van Beethoven

Ludwig van Beethoven was born in Bonn, Germany, in 1770. He came up with new, thrilling, and expressive ways of putting musical sounds together that changed the history of music forever.

Ludwig van Beethoven's best-known pieces were very different from the light, cheerful, classical music people were used to hearing at a royal gathering, dance, or party. Ludwig's music let people feel things about the joy, sadness, and stress of life.

It was sometimes very loud and exciting, and often beautiful enough to give you goose bumps all over—so it wasn't the kind of music that was going to go over very well at a polite party or dance.

In the early 1800s, European musicians, writers, and painters wanted to express the beauty and wildness of nature. This painting, by German artist Joseph Koch, shows a waterfall in Germany.

Beethoven grew up during a time in history when things were beginning to change all over Europe. This period was known as the Age of Enlightenment. For the first time in hundreds of years, writers, artists, and everyday people had new respect for education, science,

new ideas, honesty, and the beauty and wildness of nature. Also, for the first time in Europe, every person was thought of as being equally important, even if they weren't born into a wealthy or royal family. When Beethoven was a teenager, he heard that the citizens of France started a revolution against their king and queen. They decided they were tired of being very poor and treated like servants.

Beethoven thought the people of France and their leader, Napoleon, were great heroes, fighting for the freedom and rights of everyone. A few years later, Beethoven wrote music that went along perfectly with the changing times. One of his greatest compositions, the Third Symphony, is also known as the *Eroica* ("heroic") symphony. It is filled with powerful, heroic sounds and feelings. Beethoven wrote it in honor of his favorite hero, Napoleon.

A scene from the French Revolution

When Ludwig van Beethoven was born, both his father and grandfather were singers and musicians in the court of the prince of Bonn, Germany. Mr. Beethoven could tell right away that his son had a lot of musical talent. When Ludwig was only four years old, his father started teaching him to play the piano. Ludwig was so little that he had to stand on a stool to reach the keys. Unfortunately, Mr. Beethoven wasn't a very good father or teacher. He often drank too much alcohol and worked Ludwig very hard—hard

enough to be considered cruel by some
people. It seemed like Mr. Beethoven
didn't care as much about his son's
future as he did about making himself
famous by trying to become the father
of a great musician.

By the time he was eight years old, Ludwig had become a pretty good piano player. His father invited people to their home and charged them money to hear his son play. Ludwig did only a few public performances, though. Mr. Beethoven really didn't know how to teach his son properly, and Ludwig may not have been good enough yet to have people pay to hear him.

Luckily, right around this time, the prince of Bonn hired a new court organ player. Christian Neefe was an excellent musician. He heard Ludwig play, and knew he could be a great musician some day.

Christian Neefe began teaching
Beethoven in a kinder, more caring way.
Ludwig kept getting better and better.
When Ludwig was only twelve,
Christian felt comfortable enough, every
once in a while, to leave him in charge
of playing the organ and directing the
court orchestra all by himself!

When Beethoven was around 18 years old, the prince of Bonn thought it might be a good idea to show him off a little bit. He was proud of Beethoven's talent, and sent Ludwig to the city of Vienna, Austria.

Beethoven playing the piano for Mozart for the first time

Vienna in the late 1700s

Vienna was the center of music in Europe at that time. Beethoven impressed people there and got a chance to play for Vienna's most famous composer, Wolfgang Amadeus Mozart. Mozart thought Beethoven's playing was wonderful. Ludwig hoped he might be able to study with the great composer, but Ludwig's mother had become seriously ill, and he returned home to be with her.

Soon after Ludwig got back to Bonn, his mother died. Not long after that, Beethoven's baby sister died. To make things worse, Mr. Beethoven began to drink even more, and wasn't able to work any longer as a court musician. Ludwig was worried about his father and his two younger brothers, Casper and Nikolaus. He asked the prince of Bonn if he could take over as head of the Beethoven family. The prince, who knew all about Ludwig's father, agreed. Ludwig was relieved, but

found that running a house, caring for
two younger brothers, and trying to keep
his father out of trouble interfered a lot
with his music studies.

Even though the city of Bonn was an excellent place to learn about music, Ludwig van Beethoven really wanted to return to Vienna. Wolfgang Mozart had died by this time, but Ludwig was offered a chance to study with another one of the city's famous composers, Joseph Haydn.

Haydn read a musical piece written by Beethoven and arranged for him to be one of his students.

Joseph Haydn

Haydn leading a quartet in rehearsal

Ludwig gave his father enough money
to take care of Casper and Nikolaus,
and left for Vienna in 1792.

Only seven weeks later, Beethoven's
father died. Beethoven's two brothers
eventually joined him in Vienna, and he
never returned to Bonn.

When he first arrived in his new city, Ludwig learned all about classical music from Joseph Haydn and other excellent teachers. He started to compose more music and gave concerts to make money. Ludwig van Beethoven was a big hit in Vienna, not so much for his compositions at the time, but for his great piano playing. People loved to hear his imaginative playing and watch his powerful hands move quickly across the keyboard.

He gave new twists to music, and became
as popular as any rock star is today!

Beethoven had many musical successes throughout his life. Wealthy people paid him lots of money to write his wonderful music. They were amazed by how he kept coming up with new and imaginative compositions.

But Ludwig van Beethoven also had a lot of problems. First of all, he was always deeply troubled by the way his father had brought him up. In fact, some people think that the storminess between them can be heard in Beethoven's music. Secondly, he could never seem to find the right girlfriend.

Among the women who Beethoven loved, but never married, were Giuletta Guicciardi (above) and Marie-Therese von Brunswick (left).

As many times as he fell in love, things never worked out, and he never got married. Ludwig also had some problems with his brothers and their families, too. The worst thing, though, was that Beethoven began to lose his hearing just when he was starting to do his greatest work!

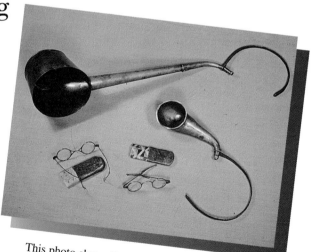

This photo shows Beethoven's eyeglasses, as well as the metal ear trumpets he used to help him hear better.

Because Beethoven had so many problems and a forceful personality, people often thought he was crabby and unfriendly. He once wrote a letter to his brothers explaining that he wasn't really a grouch. He said he sometimes ignored people because he couldn't hear them very well.

Beethoven didn't want anyone to know that someone who was supposed to be a great composer could hardly hear his own music.

Beethoven composing

Ludwig van Beethoven tried very hard not to let his problems get in the way of his work. He often had to struggle to write his beautiful string quartets, sonatas, concertos, and symphonies.

Beethoven is probably best known for his nine symphonies. A symphony is an important musical work played by an orchestra.

It usually has four parts, or movements. Beethoven's symphonies were more exciting than most of those that had been written before. He used bigger orchestras and sometimes had them play parts very loud and then very soft to get different and interesting moods.

He often used a musical theme or tune over and over, changing or disguising it, or just playing a part of it, to keep his audience guessing as to what he might do next. One of Beethoven's most famous themes is only four notes long. Those four notes may be the most exciting ever written, and you can hear them in the beginning of his Fifth Symphony.

Ludwig van Beethoven always loved nature, and spent much of his time in the peaceful countryside near his home. While he could still hear, Beethoven wrote down ideas for his music from the different sounds of the forest.

In his Sixth Symphony, also known as the *Pastoral*, Beethoven created a kind

A painting by 19th-century German Romantic painter Caspar David Friedrich

of musical story, or picture, for people to imagine while they listened to it. He gave the symphony five parts instead of the usual four, and gave each one a title that described it. The first movement is about the happy feeling you get when you arrive in the country. Then, there's a scene by a brook. The third part is the gathering

of villagers. Next is the thunderstorm.
And, finally, a song by a shepherd who
is grateful that the storm is over.

The amazing thing about the *Pastoral*
symphony is that the music is so
powerful, you almost feel like you're
actually in the middle of a beautiful

countryside, meadow, or forest—not just picturing it. In one section, Beethoven included actual bird songs he copied from the nightingales, quails, and cuckoos he heard while gathering his ideas.

Many people think that the music Beethoven wrote in his later years was his best. He seemed to have brought all his imagination, love, and power to these pieces. In his last symphony, the Ninth, Beethoven even added a chorus of singers to go along with the orchestra. Of all of Beethoven's music, this exciting symphony may do the best job of giving you goose bumps all over.

Ludwig van Beethoven lived to be 57 years old. In many of his joyous musical pieces he seemed to be saying, "Even with lots of problems, if you try hard enough, you can do anything you want, like I did." It's easy to find Beethoven's music on the radio. Libraries usually have compact discs or cassette tapes you can borrow, too. Even aliens can listen to Beethoven's music, if they're lucky enough to find *Voyager 2*. When this space probe was launched in 1977, a recording of the Fifth Symphony was included as a sample of what human beings are all about.